Rainforest

Angela Wilkes

KING*f*ISHER

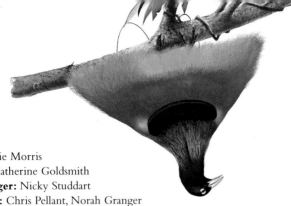

Editor: Jennie Morris
Designer: Catherine Goldsmith
DTP manager: Nicky Studdart
Consultants: Chris Pellant, Norah Granger
Indexer: Jason Hook
Production controller: Jo Blackmore
Illustrators: Lisa Alderson 8–9; **Chris Forsey** 4–5, 15*tl*, 28–29;
Ray Grinaway 6–7, 16–17, 22–23; **David Holmes** 20*tl*; **Stephen**
Holmes 17*tr*; **Ian Jackson** 24–25; **Adam Marshall** 24*tl*; **Joannah**
May 14–15, 18–19; **Terence Lambert** 21*tr*; **Simon Mendez** 10–11;
Nicki Palin 12–13; **Clive Pritchard** 18*bl*; **Bernard Robinson** 20*bl*;
Eric Robson 26–27; **David Wood** 4*bl*.
Cartoons: Ian Dicks
Picture research manager: Jane Lambert
Picture acknowledgements: **4***cl* Martin Harvey/NHPA; **7***cr* Bruce
Coleman Collection; **10***cl* Jurgen & Christine Sohns/Frank Lane
Picture Agency; **22***c* Gerald S. Cubitt/Bruce Coleman Collection;
24*bl* Alain Compost/Bruce Coleman Collection; **25***tr* Kevin
Schafer/NHPA; **27***tr* Michael Fogden/www.osf.uk.com;
29*tr* Silvestris/Frank Lane Picture Agency.

Every effort has been made to trace the copyright holders of the photographs.
The publishers apologise for any inconvenience caused.

KINGFISHER
Kingfisher Publications Plc,
New Penderel House,
283–288 High Holborn,
London WC1V 7HZ
www.kingfisherpub.com

First published by Kingfisher Publications Plc 2002
10 9 8 7 6 5 4 3 2

2TR/0501/TIMS/RNB(RNB)/128MA

Copyright © Kingfisher Publications Plc 2002

A CIP catalogue record for this book
is available from the British Library.

ISBN 0 7534 0678 0

Printed in China

J 171,539
€ 8.00

CONTENTS

ABOUT this book

Have you ever wondered how gibbons swing through trees? On every page, find out the answers to questions like this and other fascinating facts about the rainforest. Words in **bold** are explained in the glossary on page 31.

Look and Find
★ ★
angel fish

All through the book, you will see the **Look and Find** symbol. This has the name and picture of a small object that is hidden somewhere on the page. Look carefully to see if you can find it.

Now I Know...

★ This box contains quick answers to all of the questions.
★ They will help you remember all about the amazing world of the rainforest.

WHAT is a rainforest?

A rainforest is a dense, steamy forest that grows in tropical countries where it is hot all the time. Millions of giant trees grow close together, draped in exotic plants and trailing **creepers**. It pours with rain nearly every day and there are no seasons, so the trees stay green all year round. More types of plants and animals live in rainforests than anywhere else.

Gibbon

WHY do the trees grow so tall?

Rainforest trees grow very fast in the hot, wet conditions. They race with each other to reach the Sun's light, so they grow very tall. Most of them have long, thin trunks. They spread out their branches about 50 metres from the ground to form a leafy **canopy**. But some giant trees, called **emergents**, grow even taller, and tower above the rest of the forest.

Many of the smallest animals in the world, such as this tiny chameleon, live in rainforests.

Poison dart frog

Pygmy chameleon

4

That's Amazing!

Over half the known animals and plants in the world live in tropical rainforests!

Rainforests are just like giant sponges. Some of them can soak up a massive 10 m of rain every year!

Scarlet macaw

Colourful macaws and toucans live high in the forest canopy.

Morpho butterflies

Leaf-cutter ants

WHICH animals live in a rainforest?

An extraordinary variety of animals live in rainforests. They range from biting insects, poisonous frogs and snakes, to butterflies as big as birds, exotic parrots and large **apes**. Animals live at different levels in the trees, depending on where they find their food. Some roam the gloomy forest floor, while others move through the shady **understorey** or spend their whole lives high in the sunny treetops.

Now I Know...

★ A rainforest is a forest that grows in hot places where it rains a lot.

★ The trees grow very tall as they reach for sunlight.

★ A huge variety of different animals live in rainforests.

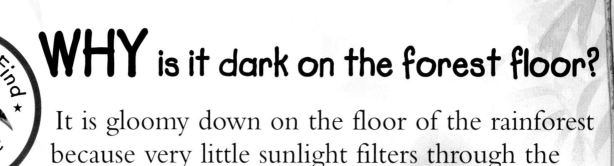

WHY is it dark on the forest floor?

★ Look and Find ★ millipede

It is gloomy down on the floor of the rainforest because very little sunlight filters through the thick canopy of leaves above. It is hot and damp and the air is still. The ground is covered in a layer of dead leaves, tangled roots and young **seedlings**. In fact, it is teeming with millions of insects and tiny creatures.

WHAT are buttress roots?

Giant rainforest trees often have enormous raised roots like wings of wood around the base of their trunks. These are called **buttress roots**. They help to prop up tall trees, just as the buttresses of a cathedral support the cathedral walls.

Poison dart frog

Army ants

Tapir

Tarantula

That's Amazing!

Columns of up to 150,000 fierce army ants march across the forest floor, attacking small animals in their way!

Buttress roots can be as tall as a small house!

WHERE do jaguars prowl?

Jaguars are the largest cats in South America and live near rivers deep in the rainforest. They usually hunt at dawn or dusk, when their patterned coats make it hard to spot them prowling through the trees. Jaguars are strong swimmers and catch fish, turtles and even crocodiles. They also climb trees in search of monkeys and sleepy sloths.

Viceroy butterflies

Heliconia flower

Poison dart frog

Jaguar

Now I Know...

★ It is dark on the forest floor as very little sunlight reaches it.

★ Buttress roots prop up tall rainforest trees.

★ Jaguars prowl near rivers in the South American rainforests.

Look and Find
cicada

HOW do plants climb trees?

Climbing plants cannot reach the forest canopy by themselves. So they cling onto trees with hooks or **tendrils** and wind their way up around tree trunks towards the sunlight. Giant woody plants called **lianas** loop from one treetop to another and send long roots like ropes back down to the ground.

Eyelash viper

Liana

WHICH vine has poisonous leaves?

The passion flower **vine** has poisonous leaves. Postman caterpillars eat them and become poisonous too, before turning into butterflies. The butterflies' red and black markings warn other animals they are poisonous.

Postman butterfly

Heliconia flower

Passion flower

Poison dart frog

That's Amazing!

The giant aroid has heart-shaped leaves wide enough for a child to go to sleep on!

Strangler figs climb down trees by winding their roots around the trunks!

WHY do leaves grow so big?

In shady parts of the rainforest, some plants grow enormous leaves so they can catch more sunlight. This helps them to grow. Leaves work best if they don't soak up water, so most leaves have waxy surfaces and points at the end called drip tips. This helps the rain to run off them easily.

Strangler fig

Cheese plant

Common lancehead

Red-eyed tree frog

Now I Know...

★ Climbing plants wind their way up trees using hooks or tendrils.
★ The passion flower vine has poisonous leaves.
★ Rainforest plants have big leaves to trap more sunlight.

WHO lives in the treetops?

Birds, monkeys, snakes and many other animals live high in the treetops. Here, the branches of the trees lace together to form a huge leafy canopy with plenty of places to shelter and nest. It is hot and sunny, and there are fruit, seeds and leaves to feed on all the year round.

Emerald tree boa

Tamandua

WHERE do oropendolas nest?

Birds called oropendolas build nests like slender string baskets that hang from the trees. Female oropendolas weave the nests out of grass-shaped leaves. They attach them to the thin tips of branches, where they will be out of reach to enemies.

That's Amazing!

The top of a rainforest tree can be as big as a football pitch!

Oropendolas build their nests near wasps' nests to scare off enemies!

Harpy eagle

Toucan

Spider monkeys

Sloth

Hummingbird

HOW do spider monkeys cling on to trees?

Spider monkeys use their arms, legs and long, strong tails to cling on to trees. They coil their tails around branches to help them hang on while they pick fruit with their hands. Beneath the tip of the tail is a patch of bare skin like your palm which helps it to grip on to things more tightly.

Now I Know...

★ Birds, monkeys, snakes and many other animals live high in the treetops.

★ Oropendolas build nests that hang from tree branches.

★ Spider monkeys use their tails to cling on to trees.

11

WHAT is an epiphyte?

High above the ground, the branches and trunks of rainforest trees are covered in plants and flowers, like a tropical garden. These plants are called **epiphytes**, or air plants. They cannot grow on the dark forest floor, but thrive high up in the treetops where there is plenty of sunlight. The epiphytes cling to the trees, using their tiny roots as anchors.

That's Amazing!

A really large bromeliad can contain as much as a whole bucketful of water!

More than 28,000 different kinds of epiphytes grow on rainforest trees!

Some flowers, such as **orchids**, are epiphytes too. They often grow in the moss that lives on branches.

12

HOW do epiphytes catch water?

Epiphytes have many ways of catching water. Some have spongy roots that dangle below branches and absorb water from the air. Others have giant, waxy leaves that funnel rainwater down to their roots. Spiky plants called **bromeliads** have leaves that overlap at the base to form small water tanks. Many plants trap dead leaves to make a damp layer of **compost** in which they can grow.

WHERE do tree frogs hide?

During the hottest part of the day, tiny tree frogs wallow in the small ponds that collect in plants, or they hide beneath damp leaves. Ponds in bromeliads attract plenty of insects for the frogs to eat. Some ponds are deep enough for frogs to lay **frogspawn** during the breeding season.

Now I Know...

★ Epiphytes are plants that grow high in the sunny treetops.
★ Epiphytes absorb water from the air or trap it in leaves.
★ Tree frogs hide in ponds inside plants or under damp leaves.

WHAT do hummingbirds eat?

★ Look and Find ★ caterpillar

Hummingbirds feed on **nectar**, a sweet juice found inside flowers. Hummingbirds do not perch on flowers to feed. Instead, they hover in front of them like helicopters, beating their tiny wings up to 90 times a second. This keeps them still enough to push their long beaks into the flowers and suck up the nectar.

That's Amazing!

The rafflesia, the biggest flower in the world, smells like rotting meat!

Bees trapped inside bucket orchids have to follow an obstacle course to escape!

Orchid

HOW do bees help orchids?

Many bees in the rainforest feed on nectar and **pollen** from orchid flowers. As they visit flowers and gather food, they carry pollen from one flower to anothe This helps the orchids to mak seeds so more orchids grow

HOW do plants trap insects?

Pitcher plants trap insects and soak up the **nutrients** from them to get their food. The plants have traps shaped like pitchers or jugs that are half full of liquid. Nectar around the rims of the pitchers attracts insects. They land on the slippery rims, then fall into the liquid inside and drown.

Pitcher plant

Tiger butterfly

Bee

Now I Know...

★ Hummingbirds feed on a juice inside flowers called nectar.

★ Bees carry pollen from one orchid flower to another.

★ Pitcher plants trap insects in their pitchers.

WHICH ants collect leaves?

Trails of leaf-cutter ants scurry up and down the tall trees of the Amazon rainforest. These ants climb trees and snip off bits of leaves, which they carry back down to their huge underground nests. There, more ants make the leaves into a mushy compost on which gardens of **fungus** grow. This fungus is food for the whole ant **colony**.

Termites

WHERE do termites live?

Millions of termites live together in colonies. Some termites build huge tree nests out of mud. Others make giant nests with tall mounds of mud above them. The mounds are chimneys for the nests down below.

Leaf-cutter
ants

That's Amazing!

A giant pangolin, a type of anteater, can pick up hundreds of ants at a time on its long, sticky tongue!

A colony of leaf-cutter ants can rob the top of a tree of all its leaves in just one day!

16

WHICH insect looks like a flower?

The flower mantis has a cunning disguise – it looks just like a pink flower. The mantis hides on an orchid, pretending to be part of the flower. It keeps very still until an insect lands nearby, then it shoots out its spiny front legs to catch it. This disguise, or **camouflage**, does not only help the mantis catch food. It also makes it hard for any of its enemies to spot it.

Flower mantis

Termite mounds

Fungus

Now I Know...

★ Leaf-cutter ants collect bits of leaves so they can grow fungus with them.

★ Termites live in huge nests made from mud.

★ The flower mantis looks just like a pink flower.

WHY do chameleons change colour?

Chameleons are lizards that live in rainforest trees. They camouflage themselves by keeping very still and changing colour to match their surroundings. This makes it hard for insects to see them. Chameleons have hollow, sticky-tipped tongues as long as their bodies and tails. If an insect comes too close, their tongues shoot out and snap them up.

That's Amazing!

Chameleons can swivel their eyes and look in two different directions at once!

South American Indians dip their hunting darts in poison from frogs to make them more deadly!

WHICH frogs are brightly coloured?

Many rainforest frogs are brightly coloured, but the most colourful of all are poison dart frogs. These tiny frogs are highly poisonous. Their bright colours and patterns act as a warning signal to animals that might eat them, such as snakes.

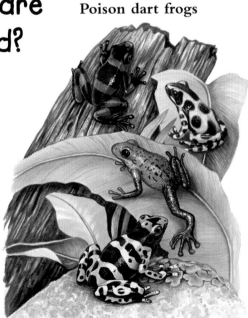

Poison dart frogs

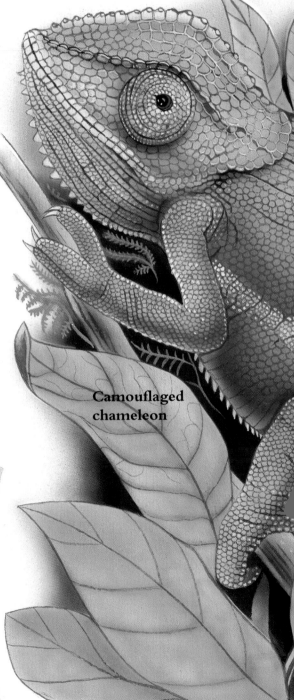

Camouflaged chameleon

18

Chameleon's long tongue

Reticulated python

HOW does a python hide?

The reticulated python lies without moving amongst the dead leaves on the forest floor. The coloured patterns on its skin help it to blend in with the leaves and camouflage it. The python waits for small animals, frogs and birds to come close. It squeezes its prey to death, before eating them whole.

Now I Know...

★ Chameleons change colour to help them catch food.
★ Poison dart frogs are brightly coloured.
★ The patterns on a python's skin help it hide in dead leaves.

WHY is a toucan's beak so big?

Toucans use their giant curved beaks to reach for juicy fruit growing on twigs too small for them to perch on. Toucans' beaks look heavy, but are really very light. Some people think that the dazzling rainbow colours and patterns on their beaks help them to signal to each other and find a mate. Toucans like company and live in flocks.

Toco toucan

WHAT do macaws and parrots eat?

Macaws and parrots eat fruit and seeds. They have powerful beaks that can crush tough nuts like a nutcracker. Parrots use their strong claws to turn nuts and seeds around while they are eating. This makes it easier to crack them open.

Scarlet macaws

That's Amazing!

Blue-crowned parrots go to sleep upside-down, like bats!

Some macaws gobble poisonous fruit, then swallow special clay to stop them getting tummy ache!

20

Toucans toss their heads back to flick food down their throats.

Male bird of paradise

Keel-billed toucan

Toco toucan

The inside edges of a toucan's beak are jagged so that it can grip berries firmly, or bite off chunks of large fruit.

WHICH birds dance and show off?

Before birds can lay eggs, they have to find a mate. Male birds of paradise have long, brightly coloured feathers on their wings or tails. They compete with each other to try to win a mate. They stand on branches and perform dances to show females how handsome they are. Some birds of paradise even hang upside-down like acrobats, fanning out their feathers and shaking them.

Now I Know...

★ A toucan uses its giant beak to reach for fruit to eat.
★ Macaws and parrots eat fruit and seeds.
★ Male birds of paradise show off their feathers to win mates.

21

★ Look and Find ★
thorn bugs

WHICH lizard can fly?

In some Asian rainforests animals can glide from tree to tree. Flying lizards have flaps of skin on their sides that open out like parachutes when they jump so they can glide to lower branches. Flying snakes launch themselves into the air and flatten their bodies. Flying frogs glide by stretching out their webbed hands and feet when they jump.

WHY do slow lorises move so slowly?

Slow lorises are small, furry animals that come out to hunt at night. They creep slowly along thin branches looking for fruit, caterpillars and insects to eat. They move very slowly so neither insects nor enemies will spot them easily.

Slow loris

Flying snake

That's Amazing!

A slow loris can 'freeze' in one position for hours at a time to avoid being seen by an enemy!

Gibbons can turn a complete circle just hanging from a tree with one hand!

HOW do gibbons swing through trees?

Gibbons are the fastest apes in the treetops. They swing from hand to hand through the trees, twisting their shoulders to reach the next branch. As they swing, they curl up their legs. This helps them go faster. Gibbons are not very big so they can hang on to small branches and reach out for fruit growing at the tips.

When a flying lizard rests on a branch, it folds its flaps of skin back along its sides.

Gibbon

Flying lizard

Flying frog

Now I Know...

★ Flying lizards in Asian rainforests can glide from one tree branch to another.

★ Slow lorises move slowly so their enemies cannot see them.

★ Gibbons swing from hand to hand through the trees.

Look and Find
cockroach

WHERE do orang-utans live?

Orang-utans are hairy orange apes that live in the swampy rainforests of Borneo. They love juicy fruit and spend their days moving from one treetop to another looking for it. Most orang-utans build two new nests a day. They make a small one for an afternoon snooze, and a bigger tree den where they sleep at night.

Orang-utan mother and baby

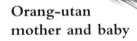

Proboscis monkey

WHICH monkey has a giant nose?

Proboscis monkeys have huge, droopy noses up to seven centimetres long. They spend hours each day sitting in mangrove trees, munching leaves. Afterwards, their tummies stick out so much that they have to go to sleep until they feel better. Proboscis monkeys also love swimming. Some of them even dive into the water from the trees.

Baby orang-utans ride with their mothers until they are strong enough to climb trees by themselves. They usually stay with their mothers until they are about eight years old, and fully grown.

Howler monkey calling

WHY do howler monkeys make so much noise?

Howler monkeys sound like leopards roaring. They live in family groups high in the treetops and howl to each other as the Sun rises. Their calls are so loud that they can be heard three kilometres away. They call to warn other groups of howler monkeys to keep away from their patch. This might be to make sure that no other monkeys take their food.

That's Amazing!

An orang-utan mother often makes herself into a bridge between trees for her baby to walk across!

Howler monkeys sunbathe in the treetops to warm up at the beginning of the day!

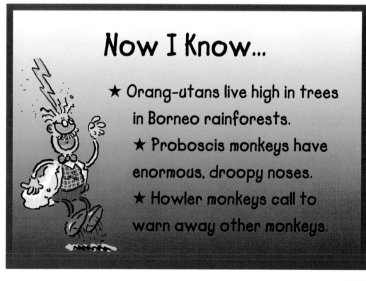

Now I Know...

★ Orang-utans live high in trees in Borneo rainforests.
★ Proboscis monkeys have enormous, droopy noses.
★ Howler monkeys call to warn away other monkeys.

25

WHICH fish have sharp teeth?

Piranhas are small fish with rows of sharp, triangular teeth. They usually eat fish, fruit and seeds, but when there is not much food they hunt in large groups called **shoals**. A shoal of piranhas is very dangerous. It can attack an animal and eat everything but its bones within a few minutes.

That's Amazing!

Anacondas can grow up to 10 m long – that's longer than a bus!

Caimans are like alligators and can float just beneath the surface of the water so other animals will mistake them for logs!

Capybaras

Caiman

Lung-fish

Discus fish

Electric eel

26

HOW does an anaconda catch its food?

Anacondas are giant snakes that live close to rivers and swamps. They are good swimmers, but they like to lie in wait for birds and animals that come down to the water to drink. An anaconda winds its huge body very tightly around prey. It squeezes the animal to death before swallowing it whole.

Anaconda

Piranhas

WHERE do mangroves grow?

Mangroves are strange trees that grow along the swampy shores and **estuaries** of rainforests. They thrive in the salty water, propped up on long roots like stilts that stick out sideways. Their roots anchor them firmly in the mud.

Now I Know...

★ Piranhas are fierce fish with sharp, triangular teeth.
★ Anacondas squeeze the animals they catch to death.
★ Mangrove trees grow along the shores of rainforests.

HOW are rainforests important?

Rainforests are important for many reasons. They are home to plants and animals that live nowhere else in the world. Many everyday foods and things we use, such as coffee, cocoa and rubber, come from rainforest plants. Other plants are used to make life-saving medicines. The huge number of trees in rainforests also affect weather all around the world. Without rainforests, a cold area could become warmer and a dry area could become wetter.

Golden lion tamarins

WHICH animals and plants are endangered?

Rainforests everywhere are being cut down. When this happens, all the plants die and many animals lose their homes and food. Some animals are also killed by hunters or captured and sold as pets. As a result, many plants and animals, from tiny insects to gorillas, are becoming very rare. Some of them, such as the golden lion tamarin, are so rare that they are in danger of dying out altogether.

Morpho butterfly

That's Amazing!

Every year, between 15 and 20 million rainforest animals are smuggled from Brazil and sold as pets!

An area of rainforest about the size of California is destroyed around the world each year!

WHY are rainforests being destroyed?

Rainforests are destroyed so people can make money from them. Many trees are cut down because their wood is valuable. Huge areas of forest are cut down by companies mining for minerals or oil. Other areas are cleared to make farms. After a few years, the land is like a desert. Nothing else will grow on it, so more forest is cut down.

Coati

Poison dart frog

Now I Know...

★ Rainforests contain valuable plants and animals, and help to control the weather.

★ Many plants and animals are becoming very rare.

★ Forests are cut down for wood, farming and mining.

RAINFOREST QUIZ

What have you remembered about the rainforest? Test what you know and see how much you have learned.

1 Where do you find rainforests?
a)   in cold places
b)   in tropical countries
c)   in dry places

2 What lives on the forest floor?
a)   monkeys
b)   birds
c)   insects

3 Which plant has poisonous leaves?
a)   strangler fig
b)   cheese plant
c)   passion flower vine

4 What are epiphytes?
a)   plants
b)   insects
c)   birds

5 What do spider monkeys like to eat?
a)   fruit
b)   worms
c)   birds

6 Which plant traps insects?
a)   pitcher plant
b)   orchid
c)   passion flower vine

7 What kind of insect builds tall mounds?
a)   ant
b)   mantis
c)   termite

8 Where do chameleons live?
a)   on the ground
b)   in trees
c)   in ponds

9 Which birds have beaks like nutcrackers?
a)   birds of paradise
b)   hummingbirds
c)   macaws and parrots

10 Which ape has orange fur?
a)   chimpanzee
b)   orang-utan
c)   gorilla

Find the answers on page 32

GLOSSARY

apes Animals like monkeys that do not have tails.

bromeliads Plants with overlapping, fleshy leaves like the top of a pineapple.

buttress roots Roots that form high supports around the bases of tall rainforest trees.

camouflage A colour, shape or pattern that hides an object. A camouflaged animal looks like its background, so it is hard to see.

canopy The part of a rainforest where the trees spread out their leafy branches like a high roof.

colony A group of the same type of animal, such as ants and termites, that live together.

compost A mixture of dead leaves that is like soil.

creepers Plants that grow along the ground or climb up supports such as trees.

emergents Huge trees that grow taller than the other trees around them in the rainforest.

epiphytes Plants that grow on trees or other plants, instead of in the ground.

estuaries Areas of water where rivers meet the sea.

frogspawn Frogs' eggs protected by jelly and laid in water.

fungus A spongy plant that is not green and does not have leaves or flowers. Fungi grow on other plants, especially dead ones.

lianas Climbing plants with woody stems.

nectar The sweet juice deep inside flowers that birds and insects like to eat.

nutrients The useful parts of food that all plants and animals need in order to grow and be healthy.

orchids Exotic flowers with waxy petals that often grow on rainforest trees. Some orchids are epiphytes.

pollen A sticky yellow powder made by flowers. Pollen has to travel or be carried from one flower to another in order for seeds to grow.

seedlings Young plants that have grown from seeds.

shoals Large groups of fish that swim and eat together.

tendrils The small, thread-like parts of climbing plants that reach out to trees and wind themselves around them.

understorey The shady, lower part of a rainforest beneath the branches of the trees.

vine A tall climbing or trailing plant with long, bendy stems.

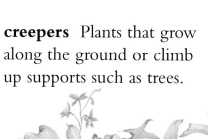

31

INDEX

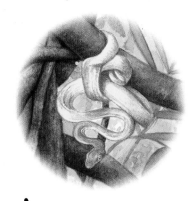

Answers to the Rainforest Quiz

★ 1 b ★ 2 c ★ 3 c ★ 4 a ★ 5 a ★ 6 a ★ 7 c ★ 8 b ★ 9 c ★ 10 b